WHO IS THE GREATEST?

ANITA GANERI

CAMBRIDGE
UNIVERSITY PRESS

UCL
Institute of Education

WHO IS THE GREATEST?

Who is the greatest sportsperson ever?

Would it be the best footballer or the tennis player winning the most championships? Or even the fastest rally driver or cyclist?

Deciding who is the greatest is not easy. It is difficult to compare sportspeople from different sports, such as a footballer to an athlete, or a gymnast to a table-tennis player.

This book looks at twelve of the greatest sportspeople. Some of them are well-known to everyone, but other names may be less familiar. All of these sportspeople have one thing in common. They became a champion in their particular sport.

WHO IS THE GREATEST?

Serena Williams	USA	Tennis
Usain Bolt	Jamaica	Sprinting
Muhammad Ali	USA	Boxing
Pelé	Brazil	Football
Sachin Tendulkar	India	Cricket
Lionel Messi	Argentina	Football
Michael Jordan	USA	Basketball
Ayrton Senna	Brazil	Formula 1 motor racing
Michael Phelps	USA	Swimming
Saïd Aouita	Morocco	Long distance running
Nadia Comaneci	Romania	Gymnastics
Deng Yaping	China	Table Tennis

SERENA WILLIAMS

HOW IS SHE GREAT?

* *Women's Tennis Association's Number 1 player.*
* *Amazingly powerful serves of over 200 km/h.*
* *Winner of a record-equalling 23 Grand Slams.*

Serena Williams began learning to play tennis when she was just three years old. She learned with her older sister, Venus. Their father taught them on their local public tennis courts in California.

Serena became a professional tennis player when she was 14. She gradually worked her way up the tennis **rankings**, beating some of the world's top players on the way. She claimed her first Grand Slam singles title, the US Open, in 1999. Success continued, and in 2002, she became World Number One for the first time. She followed this by winning all four Grand Slam titles, which was nicknamed the 'Serena Slam'. Her sister, Venus, also was one of Serena's main **rivals**, but they teamed up to win many doubles titles, including Olympic gold three times over.

Serena Williams' power and dedication to training helped her win the Grand Slam titles, like this US Open trophy.

SERENA WILLIAMS FACT FILE

Born: 1981, Michigan, USA

Grand Slam titles: 23 (14 singles, 7 doubles, 2 mixed doubles)

Olympic gold medals: 4 (singles 2012, doubles 2000, 2008 and 2012)

Overall titles: 72 singles, 23 doubles, 2 mixed doubles

She hits the ball so powerfully that it is very hard for her opponents to return the ball.

USAIN BOLT

HOW IS HE GREAT?

* World's fastest sprinter and Olympic champion in 100m, 200m and 4 x 100m relay races.
* 'Sprint double' at three Olympic Games.
* World record holder of 4 x 100m relay race.

Usain Bolt was born in a small town in Jamaica. He was sports mad, and spent hours playing cricket and football. His cricket coach noticed that he was a fast runner and encouraged him to take up track athletics.

When Usain was 15, he won the 200 metres at the World Junior Championships. By the time that he was 17, he had become the only teenager in history to run the 200 metres in under 20 seconds.

Usain won the 100 metres and 200 metres (the 'sprint double') at the 2008 Olympics in Beijing, breaking the world record in both races. He repeated this **feat** at the 2012 Olympics, and again at the 2016 Olympics.

Usain Bolt doing his signature Lightening Bolt move in the 2016 Olympic Games in Rio de Janeiro, Brazil.

USAIN BOLT FACT FILE

Born: 1986, Trelawny, Jamaica

Olympic gold medals: 8 (3 x 100 metres, 3 x 200 metres, 2 x sprint relay)

World records: 100 metres (9.58 seconds) 200 metres (19.19 seconds), sprint relay (36.84)

World titles: 11

Usain Bolt wins his races by a long way. His competitors aren't even close! His fastest recorded speed is 44.72km/h, the fastest human footspeed. His commitment to training and powerful legs have helped him become a champion.

7

MUHAMMAD ALI

HOW WAS HE GREAT?

* The only ever three-times world heavyweight champion.
* Famous for his speed, footwork and poetry.
* Claimed to 'Float like a butterfly, sting like a bee' – he moved quickly but hit hard.

Muhammad Ali started boxing in 1954, when he was 12 years old. He won a gold medal at the 1960 Olympics in Rome, then turned professional.

In 1964, he defeated a boxer called Sonny Liston to become world heavyweight champion. As the fight finished, he shouted 'I am the greatest!' to the crowd.

In 1967, Ali refused to join the US Army and his world title was taken away. He won the title back in 1974 in a famous fight in Africa. The fight was known as the 'Rumble in the Jungle'. He lost and won the world title once more before his final fight in 1981.

In 1996, Ali took part in the opening ceremony of the Centennial Olympic Games in Atlanta, USA.

MUHAMMAD ALI FACT FILE

Born: 1942, Louisville, USA

Died: 2016, Scotsdale, USA

World heavyweight champion: 1964-67, 1974-78, 1978-79

Fighting record: 56 fights, with 37 knockouts and 5 defeats

Muhammad Ali won this fight against Sonny Liston in 1964. His speed, strength and focus enabled him to overcome his opponents.

9

PELÉ

HOW WAS HE GREAT?

Probably the most famous footballer of all time.
Only player to be in the Brazil team each time they won the World Cup.
The world's most successful goal-scorer.

Pelé learned to play football with a sock stuffed with newspaper, because his family could not afford a real one. He joined Santos Football Club in 1956. By the age 16, he was Santos' top goal-scorer. He was picked for the national team, and scored his first goal for Brazil.

Aged 17, Pelé went to the World Cup in Sweden. He scored a **hat-trick** in the semi-final. He scored another two goals in the final to help Brazil beat Sweden and win the World Cup.

In 1999, Pelé was presented with the Athlete of the Century award by the International Olympic Committee. In 2013, he received the FIFA Ballon d'Or Prix d'Honneur in recognition of his career and achievements as a global **icon** of football.

Pelé holding the Jules Rimet trophy, awarded for winning the World Cup.

10

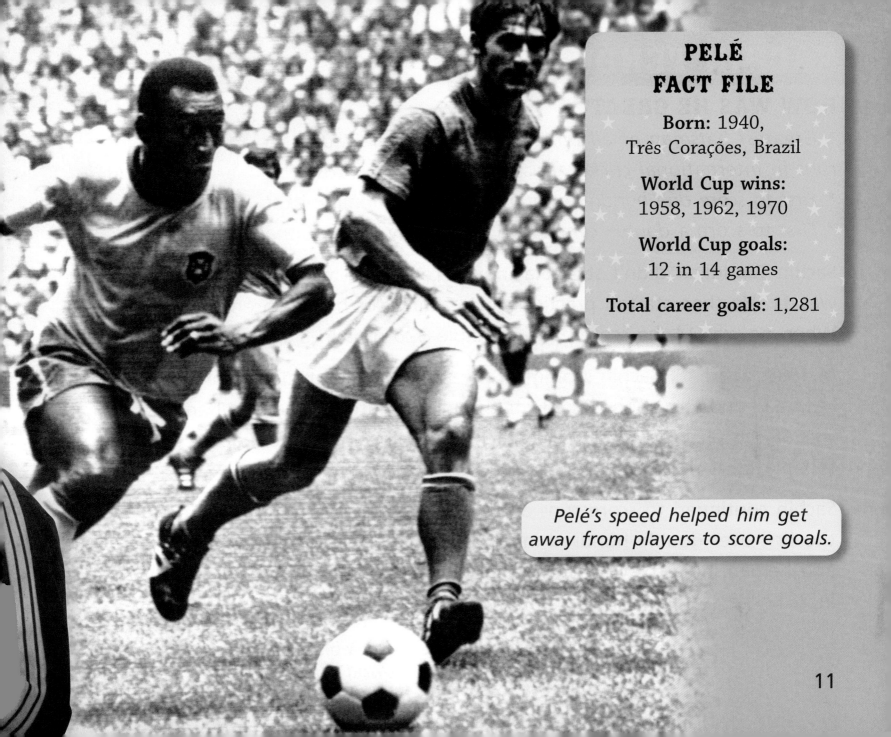

PELÉ FACT FILE

Born: 1940,
Três Corações, Brazil

World Cup wins:
1958, 1962, 1970

World Cup goals:
12 in 14 games

Total career goals: 1,281

Pelé's speed helped him get away from players to score goals.

11

SACHIN TENDULKAR

HOW WAS HE GREAT?

Greatest batsman of all time, completing over 30,000 runs in international cricket, beating all other records.

First to score one hundred centuries in international cricket.

First to score a double century in a One Day International.

Sachin Tendulkar didn't start playing cricket seriously until he was 11. He then started practising his batting for hours on end. When he was 14, he scored an incredible 326 runs in a school match.

In 1988, aged 15, Sachin scored a **century** in his debut match for Mumbai, and was soon picked for the Indian national team. When he was 16, he played his first test match, becoming India's youngest ever test player. It was against Pakistan.

Sachin continued to score runs and break records. In 2011, he scored the first ever double hundred in a One Day International match, and helped India to win the Cricket World Cup.
In 2012, he scored his hundredth international century.

Sachin Tendulkar celebrates scoring his century during a World Cup match in 2011.

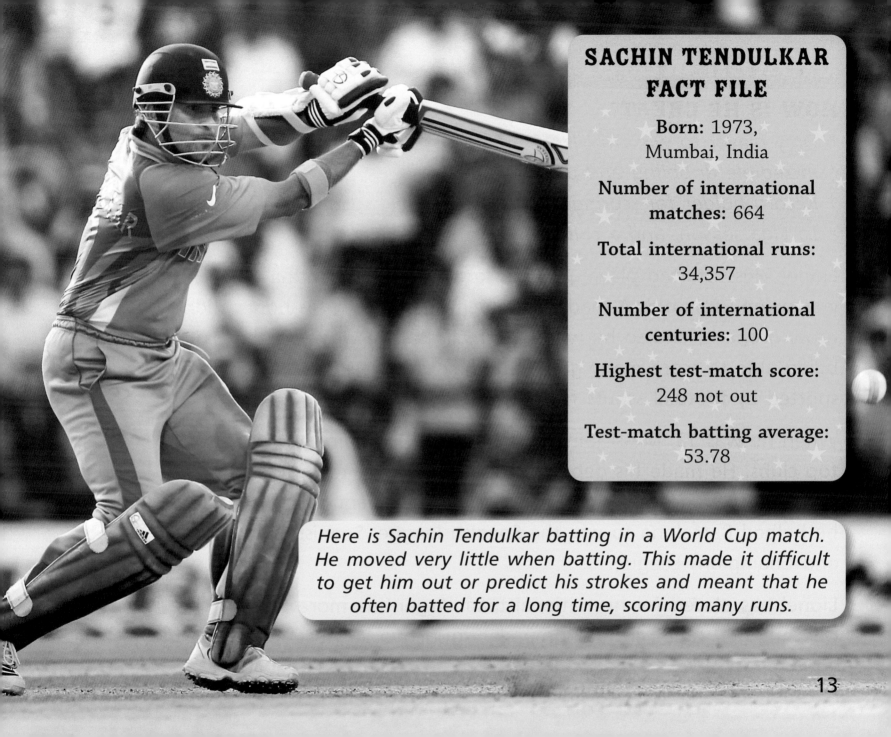

SACHIN TENDULKAR FACT FILE

Born: 1973, Mumbai, India

Number of international matches: 664

Total international runs: 34,357

Number of international centuries: 100

Highest test-match score: 248 not out

Test-match batting average: 53.78

Here is Sachin Tendulkar batting in a World Cup match. He moved very little when batting. This made it difficult to get him out or predict his strokes and meant that he often batted for a long time, scoring many runs.

LIONEL MESSI

HOW IS HE GREAT?

* Only player to win the FIFA Ballon d'Or five times.
* Incredible dribbling and passing skills.
* Record holder for scoring the most goals in La Liga overall, a La Liga season, and a club season in Europe.

Lionel Messi started playing for his local club in Argentina when he was seven years old. A medical problem meant that his bones didn't grow properly, and so he was very small. But he was also very skilful, being able to score many goals and play creatively. He was soon spotted by football scouts from Europe.

When he was 13, Messi joined FC Barcelona in Spain, one of Europe's top clubs. He made his debut for Barcelona's first team aged just 17 — the youngest player ever in the Spanish league. In 2009, he helped Barcelona to win the Spanish league, Spanish cup and Champions League.

Lionel has played for his national team Argentina more than one hundred times, including appearing in two World Cups.

Lionel Messi holding the FIFA Ballon d'Or.

LIONEL MESSI FACT FILE

Born: 1987, Rosario, Argentina

Spanish league titles: 8

Spanish cup wins: 4

Champions League wins: 4

FIFA Ballon d'Or: 2009, 2010, 2011, 2012 and 2015

Games for Argentina: 117 (58 goals)

Messi controls the ball spectacularly, sending it exactly where it is needed. Almost 90% of his passes are accurate.

15

MICHAEL JORDAN

HOW WAS HE GREAT?

* *Most famous basketball player ever.*
* *Amazing grace, power and speed - Olympic gold athlete.*
* *Highest regular average scorer - over 30 points in every game.*

In 1981, Michael went to the University of North Carolina with a basketball scholarship. He is 1.98 metres tall, and had developed a powerful **leap**. This allowed him to 'slam dunk' the ball into the basket. This avoided the risk of missing the basket when the ball is thrown in.

In 1984, Michael became a professional player with the Chicago Bulls. In his first season, he became the National Basketball Association (NBA)'s top scorer. In all, he led the Bulls to six NBA titles, and was five times the NBA's most-valuable player (MVP).

A highlight of Michael's career was playing for the US basketball team at the 1992 Olympics. The team was crammed with stars from the NBA, and was known as the 'Dream Team'.

Michael Jordan holding his 5th Maurice Podoloff Most Valuable Player Trophy in 1998.

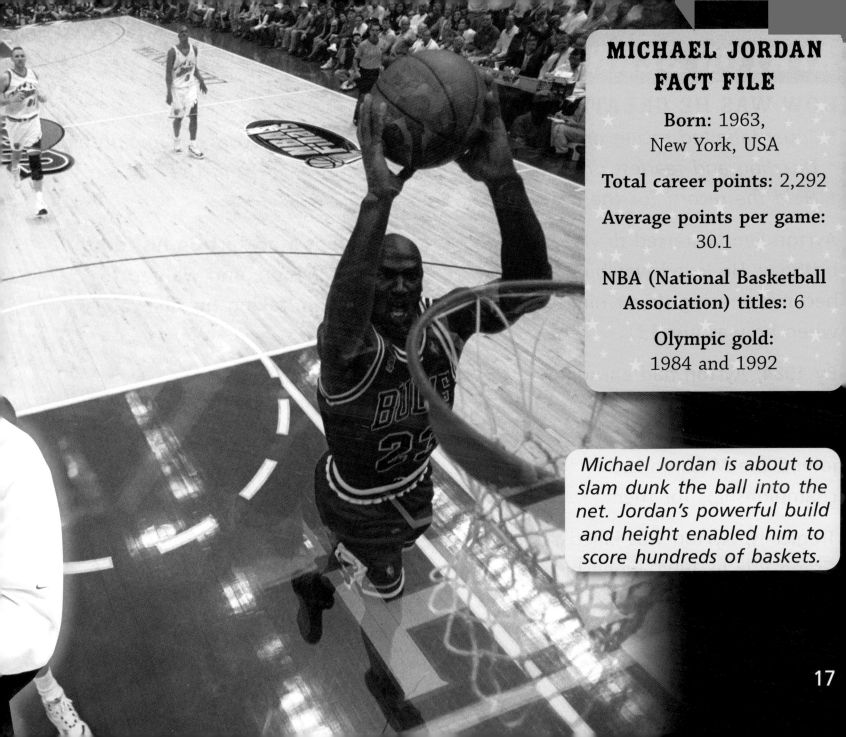

MICHAEL JORDAN FACT FILE

Born: 1963,
New York, USA

Total career points: 2,292

Average points per game: 30.1

NBA (National Basketball Association) titles: 6

Olympic gold: 1984 and 1992

Michael Jordan is about to slam dunk the ball into the net. Jordan's powerful build and height enabled him to score hundreds of baskets.

17

AYRTON SENNA

HOW WAS HE GREAT?

* Super-talented racing driver, winning three Formula One World Championships.
* Dazzling and fearless driving style, often taking the lead from the first lap.
* Held the record for the most pole positions until 2006.

Ayrton Senna started driving after his father gave him a go-kart on his fourth birthday. He loved watching Grand Prix racing on television, and wanted to become a racing driver himself. He took up kart racing, taking his first race win when he was just 13.

By 1984, Ayrton had earned a seat in a Formula 1 car through his quick reactions and driving control. His first win came in 1985, racing for Team Lotus at the Portuguese Grand Prix. Ayrton joined the McLaren racing team in 1988, and won three world championships for them.

Tragically, Ayrton was killed in an accident at the San Marino Grand Prix in 1994, when his car hit a concrete barrier at high speed. He suffered head injuries and never recovered. He was only 34 years old.

Ayrton Senna holding the trophy for winning the Grand Prix of Hungary in 1991

AYRTON SENNA FACT FILE

Born: 1960,
São Paulo, Brazil

Died: 1994,
San Marino, Italy

**Formula 1 World
Championships:**
1988, 1990, 1991

Grand Prix wins: 41

Grand Prix pole positions:
65

Ayrton Senna often won races by powering ahead on the first lap. He took risks to overtake and open up a gap while his competitors were still getting settled into the race.

MICHAEL PHELPS

HOW WAS HE GREAT?

Long course world record holder in 100m and 200m butterfly, and 400m individual medley.

Most medals in Olympic history.

First to win eight gold medals at a single Olympics.

Michael Phelps started swimming when he was seven. He was selected for the US Olympic team in 2000 when he was only 15.

In 2001, Michael set a world record time in his best swimming event, the 200-metre butterfly. This made him the youngest ever world record holder in the world of men's swimming.

At the 2004 Olympics in Athens, Michael won six gold medals, including the 100-metre and and 200-metre butterfly. Eight more golds followed at the 2008 Olympics in Beijing. Michael won more golds at London 2012. He said he would retire, but he returned for one final competition - the 2016 Olympics.

Michael Phelps with his gold medal at the Rio 2016 Olympics

MICHAEL PHELPS FACT FILE

Born: 1985, Baltimore, USA

Olympic medals: 28 (23 gold, 3 silver, 2 bronze)

World records set in career: 39

Michael Phelps, 201 centimetre arm span and extraordinarily big feet help him to swim very quickly. His long, slim body slides through the water with ease.

SAÏD AOUITA

* *World-leading middle-distance runner.*
* *Multiple world-record holder.*
* *Successful in a wide range of distances, from 800 metres to 5000 metres.*

As a child, Saïd wanted to be a footballer. But Saïd's sports coaches realised that he could be a brilliant runner when they saw how quickly he could move. Saïd trained very hard and in 1983, he was rewarded with his first big success. He won a bronze medal in the 1500 metres at the World Championships in Helsinki.

At the 1984 Olympics in Los Angeles, Saïd won gold in the 5000 metres. The following year, he broke the 5000-metre and 1500-metres world records. In 1987, he ran the first-ever sub-13-minute 5000 metres, and won the 5000 metres at the World Championships. Between 1983 and 1990, he won 115, of the 119 races he ran. Saïd retired in the early 1990s. He was voted Moroccan athlete of the 20th century in December 1999.

Born: 1959,
Kenitra, Morocco

World records:
1500 metres, 3000 metres,
5000 metres

Olympic medals: 2
(1 gold, 1 bronze)

Saïd Aouita waves to the crowd as he wins Gold in the 5000 metre final in the 1984 Olympic Games. His hours of training and exceptional speed and **stamina** have paid off.

NADIA COMANECI

HOW WAS SHE GREAT?

* Scored first-ever perfect 10 at the 1976 Olympics.
* Won the Romanian Nationals at just 8 years old.
* First to perform many gymnastics moves.

Nadia Comaneci took up gymnastics after a coach saw her doing cartwheels in her school playground and recognised her talent. She was just 13 when she competed in Romania's Junior Gymnastics Championships. A year later, she won the same competition. In 1975, Nadia won four gold medals and one silver medal in the European Championships.

Nadia became famous as a 14 year old at the 1976 Olympic Games in Montreal. Her faultless performance on the uneven bars earned her the perfect score of 10 from the judges. This had never happened before in any gymnastic event. She went on to record six more perfect scores, and won three gold medals. More golds followed at the 1980 Olympics. Nadia retired in 1984.

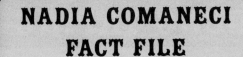

Nadia Comaneci is performing her Perfect 10-scoring sequence in the 1976 Olympic Games. Her competitive spirit kept her motivated throughout the hours of grueling training.

25

DENG YAPING

HOW WAS SHE GREAT?

Overcame her short height to become one of the world's best table tennis players.

18 times World Champion.

World number one for eight years.

Deng Yaping picked up a table-tennis bat for the first time when she was five years old. She was only eight when she won her first junior championship. At 13, she won the junior national championships for the whole of China. By then, she was regularly beating many top adult players.

Deng was soon good enough to play in China's national team, but the coaches thought she was too short. However, they soon recognised her talent and let her in, and she won the women's doubles world title. Success in the world singles followed in 1991. She kept going strong, winning gold in both singles and doubles at the 1992 and the 1996 Olympics. She also won six world titles along the way.

After retiring, Deng was a member of the International Olympic Committee. She helped to organise the Beijing Olympics in 2008.

Deng Yaping at the Beijing Olympics in 2008.

**DENG YAPING
FACT FILE**

Born: 1973
Zhengzhou, China,

Olympic gold medals: 4
(two single; two doubles)

World titles: 14
(9 gold; 5 silver)

Deng Yaping's incredible speed and accuracy enabled her to win many matches.

SO, WHO IS THE GREATEST?

So, which sportsperson is the greatest? It may be someone who is not in this book.

It can be hard to make a decision. What facts should be taken into account? Perhaps how many medals they have won, or how many world records they have broken? Perhaps they spent many years training, or they were born with a special skill? Either way, sports fans spend hours arguing about their favourites!

The sportspeople in this book are all great in their own rights. They started out as beginners and reached the top in their sports. And they are all the greatest in somebody's eyes.

century	score of 100
feat	achievement
hat trick	scoring 3 goals
icon	someone very much looked up to
leap	jump very high
rankings	position on a list of scores
rivals	competitors
stamina	ability to keep going

INDEX

WHO IS THE GREATEST? ANITA GANERI

Teaching notes written by Sue Bodman and Glen Franklin

Using this book

Content/theme/subject

Young sports lovers will enjoy this book which draws together some of the greatest sportsmen and women of all time, and poses the reader a challenging question: which one is the greatest of all? The book explores each sportsperson's life and achievements, supported by high quality photography and a host of fascinating facts, making this an interesting non-fiction read.

Language structure

- Elements of biography and journalistic writing are employed.
- Sentences are more becoming complex, but with clear structural support and effective punctuation choices to aid comprehension.

Book structure/visual features

- A set format and layout is employed to explore the life and achievements of each sportsperson featured.
- The author sets a purpose for reading, in seeking to establish who is the greatest sportsperson ever, and returns to this question in the concluding part of the book.

Vocabulary and comprehension

- Appropriate technical vocabulary is used, specific to each of the sports represented, such as 'Grand Slam' (p.4), 'slam dunk' (p.16), 'pole position' (p.19).
- Expressive language ('power and dedication to training', p.4; 'he scored an incredible 326 runs' p.12) is used to build mood and to position the reader.

Curriculum links

History – This book covers a range of different sports. Children may wish to focus on one particular sport such as football or cricket, and research the 'greatest' in each chosen field.

Maths – Greatness in sport is often judged by measurement – highest, fastest, longest, strongest. Chart and measure the children's results as they try out different athletic activities in the school gym or playground.

Learning outcomes

Children can:

- consider the impact of adverbs and adverbial phrases, noticing authorial intent to position the reader
- distinguish between fact and opinion in reading
- analyse how texts can be organised differently, suggesting reasons for these differences.

Planning for guided reading

Lesson One: Text organisation and authorial intent

Give a book to each child, and ask them to read the title and the blurb. The children will probably be very keen to tell you their favourite sportsperson! In this book, the question is which sportsperson is the greatest.

Turn to p.2 and ask the children to read the text quietly to themselves. Note the rationale for why these particular people have been selected for inclusion: 'They became a champion in their particular sport'. Discuss what is meant by 'champion'.

On p.3 and look at the list of sportsmen and women represented. Choose a sportsperson and ask the children to find that page. If there are any from your particular country or region, this might be a good place to start. For example, say to the children: *I really like watching the tennis, and I think Serena Williams is a brilliant tennis player. But I wonder if she is the greatest?*

Turn to pp.4-5. Explore the layout of these two pages. Note the functions of the different passages of text, including the biographical information in the main text, the fact file and the descriptive captions. Discuss how helpful this layout is in providing clear information to the reader.

Draw attention to the vocabulary the author uses to describe Serena Williams. Note that the word 'powerful' or 'powerfully' is used several times across the two-page spread, and how this repetition serves to reinforce the point. Discuss the biographical detail which draws attention to Williams' early life, seeking to provoke an emotional response from the reader.